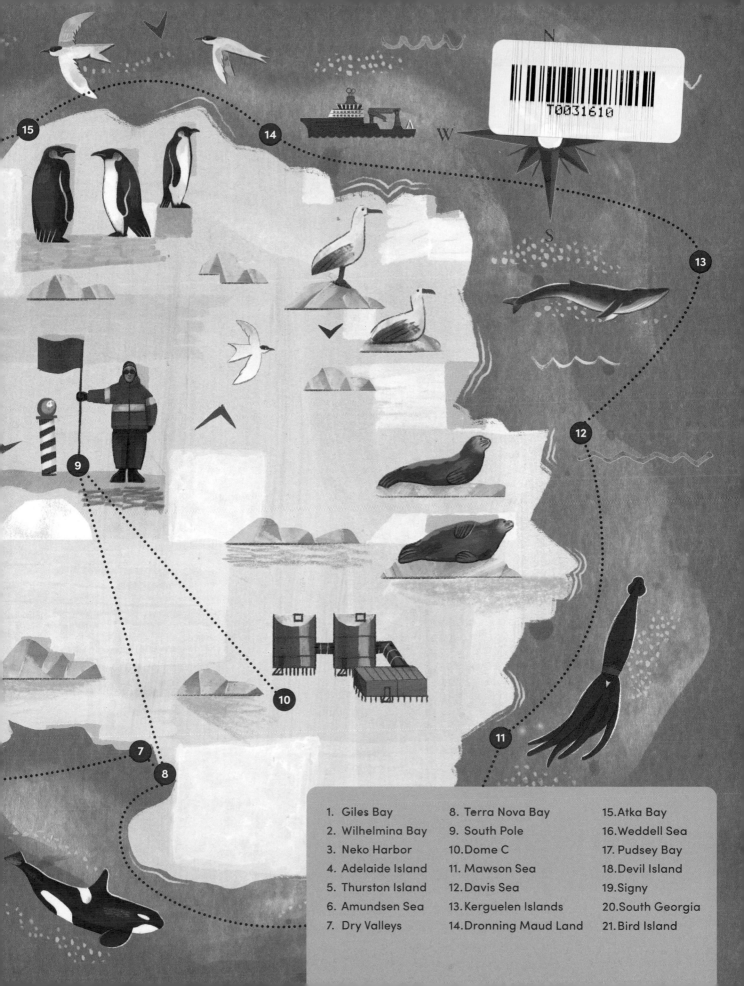

1. Giles Bay
2. Wilhelmina Bay
3. Neko Harbor
4. Adelaide Island
5. Thurston Island
6. Amundsen Sea
7. Dry Valleys
8. Terra Nova Bay
9. South Pole
10. Dome C
11. Mawson Sea
12. Davis Sea
13. Kerguelen Islands
14. Dronning Maud Land
15. Atka Bay
16. Weddell Sea
17. Pudsey Bay
18. Devil Island
19. Signy
20. South Georgia
21. Bird Island

FOR CATO AND XANDER
- H.S _and_ K.H

First edition published in 2024 by Flying Eye Books Ltd.
27 Westgate Street, London, E8 3RL.

Text © Helen Scales and Kate Hendry
Illustrations © Rômolo D'Hipólito

Every attempt has been made to ensure any statements written as fact have been checked to the best of our abilities. However, we are still human, thankfully, and occasionally little mistakes may crop up. Should you spot any errors, please email info@nobrow.net.

Edited by Sara Forster
Designed by Sarah Crookes

1 3 5 7 9 10 8 6 4 2

Published in the US by Flying Eye Books Ltd.
Printed in China on FSC® certified paper.

ISBN: 978-1-83874-882-1
www.flyingeyebooks.com

HELEN SCALES • KATE HENDRY • RÔMOLO D'HIPÓLITO

SCIENTISTS IN THE WILD
ANTARCTICA

FLYING EYE BOOKS

CONTENTS

WELCOME TO ANTARCTICA

If you head south anywhere in the world, eventually you'll reach an enormous, ice-covered continent. It's the coldest, windiest, driest place on Earth. This is Antarctica.

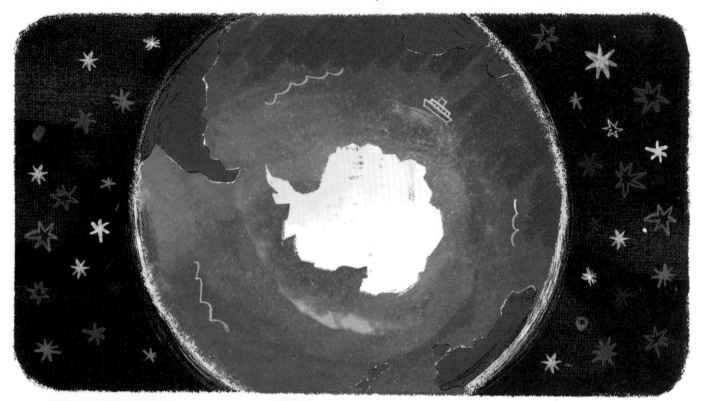

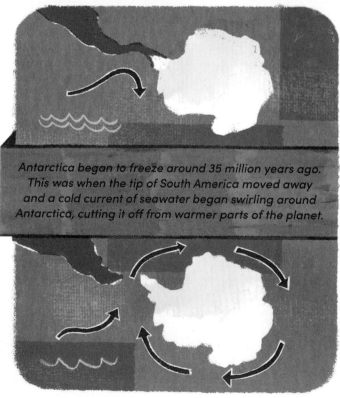

Antarctica began to freeze around 35 million years ago. This was when the tip of South America moved away and a cold current of seawater began swirling around Antarctica, cutting it off from warmer parts of the planet.

Antarctica facts

- Antarctica is the land that lies at the South Pole and is mostly covered in a massive sheet of ice, 1.24 miles deep (on average) and 5.5 million mi^2 in size. The ice sheet holds more than half of all the world's fresh water. Today there's only one other ice sheet, which covers the island of Greenland near the North Pole.

- Antarctica's ice sheet creeps over the edges of the land onto the sea, forming huge ice shelves. Hundreds of giant rivers of ice, known as glaciers, run into the sea.

- The Antarctic region is made up of Antarctica, the surrounding ice shelves, glaciers and sea, plus nineteen nearby islands and archipelagos.

- Despite the extreme conditions on the land and in the sea, the Antarctic is home to all kinds of wildlife.

Quest for a southern continent

No humans have lived permanently on Antarctica. Eight hundred years ago, Māori people called Ngāi Tahu, voyaged to islands hundreds of miles south of New Zealand, but there's little proof they went any closer to Antarctica.

For centuries, Europeans were convinced there was a huge continent at the South Pole. They called it Terra Australis Incognita, the "unknown southern continent" and it took a long time to find. Explorers from Russia set eyes on the Antarctic ice sheet on January 27, 1820. Three days later, British explorers saw the tip of the Antarctic Peninsula.

After that, many more people from around the world came to Antarctica, mainly to hunt seals and whales for their fur and oil.

Today, no one country can claim ownership of Antarctica. The Antarctic Treaty is an important international pact among over fifty countries that all agree Antarctica needs to be protected from environmental harm. It is now a place for peace and science . . .

EXPEDITION ANTARCTICA

Seven scientists have formed a team on board the *Noto* to study the changing environment and wildlife around Antarctica. They come from different countries that are members of the Antarctic Treaty and they all have special skills.

Hallå. I'm Ari Larsson. I'm co-chief scientist of the expedition.

Hi. I'm Michelle Mhlongo. I'm co-chief scientist with Ari.

Hola. My name is Javier Contreras. I can't wait to see the emperor penguins!

Annyeong! I'm Ahn Ji-hae. Call me Ji-hae.

Ari studies glaciers, sea ice, and other forms of ice. They want to understand how ice is changing as the sea gets warmer and how this affects the rest of the ocean.

Michelle is a marine biologist. She studies all kinds of creatures that live in the ocean and is especially interested in ecosystems on the seabed. Her job is also to pilot the deep-sea diving submersible.

Javier is an ornithologist— a biologist who studies birds. He specializes in birds that spend a long time at sea, like penguins and albatrosses. He is also an ecologist—a scientist who studies how different species live together in ecosystems.

Ji-hae is a chemical oceanographer. She is an expert in the nutrients found in seawater that feed algae. She will also be studying the temperature and saltiness of seawater, and the strength of ocean currents.

Oscar is a marine biologist who specializes in studying mammals like seals and whales. He has studied them in many places around the world, including Galápagos, but this is his first trip to one of the poles. On this expedition he's investigating what various marine mammals get up to down beneath Antarctica's sea ice.

Jojo is the technician and data scientist on the expedition. Her job is to look after all the technical equipment and make sure all the scientific data is properly organized and safely stored.

Lara is a physicist and is particularly interested in how the atmosphere impacts life on Earth. She specializes in taking measurements of the atmosphere all around Antarctica to help with weather forecasting. She is also on the *Noto* to study longer term climate change.

WELCOME ABOARD THE *NOTO*

This is the research vessel, *Noto*, an ice-strengthened ship about 328 feet long that will take our team of scientists on a journey all around the Antarctic continent and its islands.

Kia Ora! I'm Captain Nyree Paewai. Welcome to the *Noto*.

1. Dry lab
2. Wet lab
3. Deck
4. Galley/mess
5. Bridge
6. Life rafts
7. Cabin
8. Engine room
9. Deep-diving submersible
10. Autonomous Underwater Vehicle or AUV
11. Glider
12. Hull (strengthened so it can push through sea ice)

Zero carbon

The *Noto* is a brand-new, zero-carbon ship. Instead of burning fossil fuel, it's powered by ammonia, a much cleaner chemical that doesn't release any greenhouse gases. There is no single-use plastic on board and the team recycle everything they can. As part of the Antarctic Treaty, anyone visiting Antarctica must not leave anything behind, but take everything back with them (even the contents of the toilets!).

Noto *is short for* notothenioid, *the scientific name for one of the Antarctic's ice-proof animals, the Antarctic icefish.*

ANTARCTIC EQUIPMENT

It's important to stay warm and dry in Antarctica, one of the coldest and windiest places on Earth! To work there, scientists bring different types of clothing and equipment to wear depending on what they're doing.

The sun's ultraviolet rays are very strong in Antarctica, so everyone grabs a pair of sunglasses and sunscreen before heading outside.

Hard hat with ear warmers (because a lot of heat is lost through the head)

Sunglasses

Waterproof thermal suit

Life jacket

Strong deck boots

Underwater camera

Regulator and spare regulator adapted for ice diving (which won't easily freeze)

Hood

Air tank

Buoyancy jacket

Weight belt

Dive computer

Gloves

Underwater flashlight

Dive slate and pencil

Undersuit (like a fluffy jumpsuit) to keep warm

Dry suit

Sea surface temperatures around Antarctica go down to around 28.76°F

On deck

When members of the *Noto* team work outside on deck they wrap up warm.

Ice diving

To study the top almost 100 feet of the seas around Antarctica, the dive team uses scuba gear specially adapted for ice diving.

On the ice

The team can walk out onto the sea ice (provided it's thick enough!). This means that they can study the wildlife that like to haul out of the sea, like penguins and seals. They can also lower their science equipment through holes in the ice to take measurements of the water underneath.

But they have to be extra careful! Falling through the ice into freezing water can cause hypothermia—a dangerous drop in body temperature. The *Noto* team wears extra-warm, waterproof survival suits. They tie themselves together with strong ropes, and carry ice axes, so they can pull out anyone who falls in!

Deep under the ice

The *Noto* has different kinds of equipment to study deeper water, either in person or with machines that go down on their own.

Deep-diving Submersible, *Kiwa*

Depth: Down to almost 4 miles

Autonomous Underwater Vehicle (AUV), *Mirounga*

Depth: Down to almost 4 miles

This diving robot steers itself underwater for days and weeks at a time. It has sensors and cameras on board to gather information.

Glider
Depth: Down to 3,081 feet

GUIDE TO ANTARCTIC LIFE

All sorts of wildlife live in and around Antarctica; on the frozen continent itself, on the nearby islands, and in the surrounding waters of the Southern Ocean. Some animals live here permanently. Others are visitors that visit every year. Michelle and Javier tell the rest of the team about the species they will find during the *Noto* expedition.

The ecosystems of Antarctica are linked in many ways to ice.

Many of Antarctica's species are at risk from climate change because their cold, icy world is changing fast.

Seals use sea ice to rest on and raise their pups.

Lots of animals eat krill, including seals, penguins, albatrosses, squid, and whales.

Small swimming animals, called krill, spend winters under the sea ice, grazing on layers of green algae.

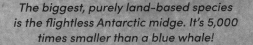
The biggest, purely land-based species is the flightless Antarctic midge. It's 5,000 times smaller than a blue whale!

Emperor penguins raise their chicks on sea ice.

Penguins climb onto chunks of ice to rest and shed their feathers.

Even the biggest animals that ever lived—blue whales—come to Antarctica to feast on krill.

Extinction categories:

Scientists assess species and work out how close they are to extinction, based on how many are alive, how fast the population is shrinking, and the health of their habitat.

LC **Least Concern**
Unlikely to go extinct any time soon

NT **Near Threatened**
Close to being at high risk of extinction in the future

V **Vulnerable**
High risk of extinction

EN **Endangered**
Very high risk of extinction

CE **Critically Endangered**
Extremely high risk of extinction

EW **Extinct in the Wild**
Only alive in captivity

EX **Extinct**
No living members left

? **Unassessed**

17

TINY CLIMATE CRITTERS

The *Noto* team begin its expedition along the West Antarctic Peninsula, a long finger of land that points towards South America. Their first stop is Giles Bay where they study tiny algae in the water and the tiny animals that eat them. These creatures may be small but the scientists want to work out how big a role they play in helping to absorb carbon out of the atmosphere.

Antarctic krill
Euphausia superba

Size: Around 2 inches
Lifespan: 6 years
LC Least Concern

– Giles Bay –

Giles Bay was named after British scientist Dr. Katharine Giles.

Counting krill

Ji-hae and Michelle use very fine mesh nets, called plankton tows, to catch krill and algae. Later on, the team spends hours and hours counting them!

Krill are a type of small crustacean. They can live in huge swarms in waters around Antarctica. Scoop up a bucket of seawater, and there can be as many as one hundred krill in it.

Carbon dioxide gas in the atmosphere gets absorbed by algae. Then the carbon gets passed on to krill that eat the algae. By studying chemicals inside krill, Ji-hae finds out that they put lots of carbon into their poop which falls quickly to the seabed, taking the trapped carbon with it.

Catching sinkers

Sediment traps have been sitting in the ocean for more than a year waiting for the *Noto* team. These gadgets collect particles that sink down through the water, such as dead algae and krill poop. Ji-hae pulls up the traps to see what's in them. She finds lots of krill poop and works out that they are very important indeed!

The samples are stored on the ship until they can be studied back home.

Climate superstars

Krill play a big part in resisting climate change by sending masses of poop into the deep sea where it stays for thousands of years. This helps to take up some of the carbon dioxide humans are releasing which trap the sun's heat in the atmosphere. Roughly three quarters of all the carbon buried in the seabed around the Antarctic Peninsula comes from krill poop.

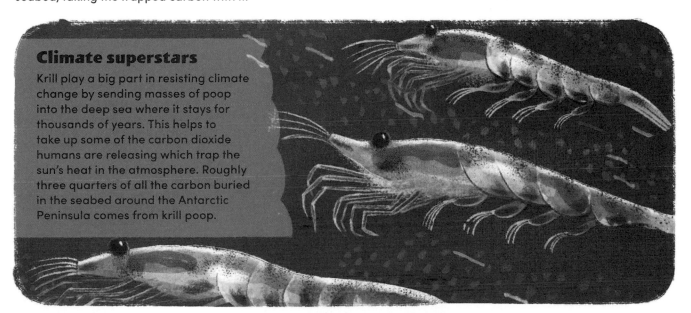

ICE DIVERS

The *Noto* sails into Wilhelmina Bay and the team spots a large pod of at least thirty minke whales. Oscar quickly gets ready to try and to fix a tag onto one of them so he can find out more about how they hunt for krill. But it's not easy—minkes are fast!

Oscar and Michelle carefully steer the inflatable boat to get closer to the pod. Luckily the whales are busy hanging out together and ignore the scientists. Just before one whale dives under the ice, Michelle reaches in with a long pole and fixes a tag to its back. A few nail-biting minutes later and the whale resurfaces with the expensive tag still attached!

Antarctic minke whale
Balaenoptera bonaerensis

Size: 26-30 feet
Lifespan: 50+ years
NT Near Threatened

The tag measures depth, speed, and position which together indicate how often the whale opens its mouth and gulps a huge mouthful of krill. These whale movements are called lunges. Oscar discovers that minke whales dive in three ways—including one that's completely different to any other whale.

How minke whales dive

Dive type 1: Swim near the surface. One to two lunges per dive.

Dive type 3: Skim under the sea ice. Twenty four lunges per dive, or once every 3 seconds! (Blue whales lunge four times per dive, and humpback whales lunge 12 times per dive.)

Dive type 2: Plunge down to 328 feet. Fifteen lunges per dive.

Minke whales are small and agile. They're the most common species to spot around Antarctica.

Temperatures along the West Antarctic Peninsula have been going up five times faster than the rest of the world and the sea ice is shrinking. This is affecting penguins in many ways but some species are coping better than others. The *Noto* team arrives in Neko Harbor to find out why gentoo penguins here are doing well.

Around 1,000 pairs of gentoo penguins are tending their chicks in rocky nests on the shore of Neko Harbor.

Penguin survivors

Across Antarctica, gentoo penguins are thriving and moving into new territories. Scientists think this could be because gentoos are not too fussy about what they eat. And they don't like ice very much, but prefer to go fishing in open water. Sea ice is shrinking and gentoos are moving further south along the peninsula.

Gentoo penguin
Pygoscelis papua

Size: 3 feet
Lifespan: 15–20 years
LC Least Concern

Penguin watch

Ari sends up a drone to take pictures of the whole colony of gentoos. Later on, they'll count how many birds there are.

Jojo checks on the time-lapse cameras that watch over the colony. The cameras have been taking one picture every hour, from dawn until dusk, ever since the penguins arrived to lay their eggs. The pictures will help the team see how the penguins are feeding and how fast the chicks grow.

Javier carefully scoops up samples of penguin poop. These are very useful droppings. They show the scientists what penguins eat, what condition the birds are in, if they are stressed, and if they are carrying any diseases.

Chinstrap penguin
Pygoscelis antarcticus

Size: Almost 2.5 feet
Lifespan: 20 years
ⓛⓒ Least Concern

– Neko Harbor –

Neko Harbor was named after a Scottish whaling ship.

ICE STATION ANTARCTICA!

A lot of science around Antarctica is done by scientists living in research stations on land. Some science bases are only open in summer but a few are open all year, throughout the long, dark Antarctic winter. The *Noto* team drops into one of the research stations on Adelaide Island to assist the resident scientists.

Chasing clouds

Jojo and Lara release a weather balloon, which carries sensors as it floats high up to study the clouds.

Clouds around Antarctica are different from everywhere else on the planet, partly because the air here is so clean. It's important to know how these clouds form and behave because they play a key role in climate change by reflecting the sun's energy back into space.

Sea sampling

Ji-hae is measuring the temperature and saltiness of the water in the bay and collecting water samples to measure different chemicals. This will help the scientists figure out how nearby melting glaciers are changing the seawater and conditions for sea life, such as algae.

Long-term science

One reason it's good to work on research stations is because scientists can collect data from the same places year after year. Data collected over a very long period of time helps track how the ocean and climate are changing.

There are seventy research stations around Antarctica, run by twenty-nine countries.

– Adelaide Island –

Adelaide Island is about 86 miles long, just under 23 miles wide and 1 mile high at its highest point.

A HIDDEN WORLD UNDER THE ICE

The dive team plunge through a hole drilled into the thick sea ice and plunges through what feels like a portal into a secret world.

There are intricate animals swimming and drifting around, and colorful creatures crawling across the busy seabed.

Ice stalactites, also known as brine icicles or brinicles, hang down from the ceiling of ice. Brinicles form when super-cold, super-salty water seeps through the sea ice and quickly sinks, freezing the seawater around them in long spears.

When brinicles touch the bottom, they create frozen rivers that spread across the seabed. When this happens, starfish and sea urchins have to get out of the way, otherwise they freeze instantly!

27

HOW STRESSED ARE SEA SPIDERS?

The dive team has carefully collected several giant sea spiders from the seabed and brought them into the *Noto*'s dry lab. They want to study how the spiders might be affected as the sea carries on getting warmer due to climate change.

Spider tests

Michelle places each spider in an aquarium with seawater of a certain temperature. She turns each spider over onto its back.

28.76°F **39.2°F** **48.2°F**

Some are kept at 28.76°F, the temperature sea spiders expect in the wild.

Others are kept in warmer water, at 39.2°F.

And some are even warmer, at 48.2°F.

Then she times how long it takes for it to turn itself the right way up. The more stressed a spider is, the longer it takes to turn over.

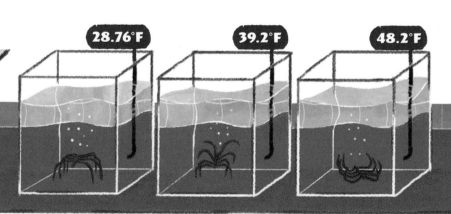

28.76°F **39.2°F** **48.2°F**

Michelle sees that the warmer spiders turn themselves over between ten and twenty times slower than the cold ones.

As she expected, the warmer the water, the more stressed sea spiders become.

28

The trouble with being big

Michelle also predicted that bigger sea spiders would get more stressed by the warmth than smaller ones. That's because sea spiders don't breathe with gills, but through the outer layer of their skin, called the cuticle. Bigger spiders have a smaller area of cuticle, compared to the large volume of their body. So they might find it harder to breathe than smaller spiders, especially in warm water that holds less oxygen than cold water.

To Michelle's surprise, the bigger sea spiders don't always take longer to turn themselves over.

19.7–27.6 inches   *3.94 inches*

When she looks at them under a microscope, she sees the bigger spiders have lots of tiny holes in their cuticle which help them absorb more oxygen and breathe.

Her study shows that it's not a simple matter to work out which animals will be hit the hardest by climate change. Some sea spiders will suffer more, but not necessarily the biggest ones.

When the tests are finished, Michelle carefully puts the sea spiders back in the sea.

Sea spiders are not arachnids, but close relatives of true spiders, scorpions, ticks, and mites.

Giant sea spider
Colossendeis colossea

Size: About 28 inches
Lifespan: Unknown
(?) Unassessed

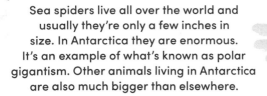

Sea spiders live all over the world and usually they're only a few inches in size. In Antarctica they are enormous. It's an example of what's known as polar gigantism. Other animals living in Antarctica are also much bigger than elsewhere.

SURVIVAL STRATEGIES

Animals have evolved all sorts of special adaptations to survive the extreme conditions in Antarctica. From feathers to fat, long journeys to long snoozes, there are many ways of coping with life on the frozen continent.

Fancy feathers

Key to the penguins' survival in Antarctica are their feathers. Emperor penguins have many different types of feathers which keep them warm when they're diving deep underwater and when the temperature out on the ice plummets to -40°F.

Contour feathers form a stiff, waterproof, windproof layer on the outside. There are lots of contour feathers on emperor penguins' bellies, which cushion them when they toboggan along over rough snow.

Every year, emperor penguins shed their old feathers and grow a new coat to make sure they stay in good condition.

Total number of contour feathers = 30,000.

Afterfeathers are downy fluff stuck to contour feathers.

Plumules are downy bits attached directly to the skin. Together, they trap air in an insulating layer.

Total number of afterfeathers + plumules = 150,000.

Blubbery goodness

Many animals living in cold seas have a thick layer of fat under their skin, called blubber, which helps to keep them warm. Weddell and crabeater seals have blubber around 2 inches thick. Blubber isn't just for warmth, it's also an important source of food. When there's not much around to eat, seals can survive by using the energy stored in their blubber.

Long-distance migrations

Some animals don't spend the whole year in Antarctica but avoid the harshest time by heading north. Arctic terns are some of the most extreme—they fly all the way from the Arctic to Antarctica every year, a round trip of almost 22,000 miles! By switching between the polar summers in the north and south, Arctic terns see more sunlight than any other animal on the planet.

Sleepy fish

Some Antarctic fish survive the winters thanks to a fishy version of hibernation. They don't fall fast asleep, but they swim much less and grow slowly. They do this probably because it's hard to find prey in the dark, so instead they sit still and save energy.

THE ART OF NOT FREEZING

In the 1960s, a scientist called Art DeVries spent a lot of time diving in Antarctica. For hours and hours he watched fish and noticed something very strange—they don't freeze. Even when a fish sits on ice or squeezes into an icy crevice to hide from seals, it doesn't turn into a block of ice.

Art took samples of fish blood and worked out that it freezes at 28.4°F—slightly below the freezing point of salty seawater.

How, he wondered, is this possible? What's their secret to not freezing?

Art solved the puzzle when he found a special kind of protein in fish blood that works like antifreeze. It stops ice crystals from growing bigger.

As well as having antifreeze flowing through their blood, Antarctic fish also cover their skin in a layer of antifreeze slime which stops them from getting smothered in ice. They can even get rid of ice crystals from their body by pushing them out in their poos.

Following Art's discovery, other scientists found types of antifreeze in all sorts of animals and plants, from trees to beetles, moths to plankton.

Antarctic icefish (the Notothenioids) and Arctic cod make almost identical forms of antifreeze, even though they're not close relatives and they live at opposite poles.

People can now make synthetic versions of fish antifreezes and use them to make delicious ice cream, with small, smooth ice crystals.

DeVries Glacier in Antarctica, near the Ross Sea, is named after Art.

AN ANCIENT LOST WORLD

Antarctica has not always been icy and frozen. One hundred million years ago, during the Cretaceous period, Earth was much warmer than today. Antarctica was covered in lush rainforests inhabited by dinosaurs.

Enormous titanosaurs reached up into the canopy to munch leaves. Stomping across the forest floor were stocky, armor-plated dinosaurs with spikes on their backs, called *Antarctopelta*.

The carbon dioxide in the atmosphere during the Cretaceous period came from lots of erupting volcanoes.

All these animals are now extinct.

Darting through the undergrowth were smaller plant eaters, the *Trinisaura*. Chasing after them were powerful predators including *Morrosaurus*, and soaring above the trees were giant, flying reptiles, the pterosaurs.

Life in the Cretaceous Southern Ocean was also completely different than today. Giant marine reptiles were cruising around. *Kaikaifilu* was a predator with powerful snapping jaws and measured at least thirty-two feet long—bigger than great white sharks. There were *Elasmosaurus* with ridiculously long necks, paddling along with four giant flippers. Swimming around were relatives of octopuses and squid, called ammonites.

Just like today, Antarctica in the Cretaceous period had long, dark winters. And somehow the forests and animals survived. Scientists haven't yet found any evidence that dinosaurs hibernated, but maybe they huddled together to keep warm like male emperor penguins do. Some dinosaurs living near the South Pole had huge eyes, giving them good night vision.

Antarctica's trees used stores of energy to get through the polar night.

Then during the summer they could make lots more food by harnessing energy from the sun which shone for twenty-four hours a day.

We know about Antarctica's ancient plants and animals from fossils, including a lot found on James Ross Island off the Antarctic Peninsula. Cores of mud drilled from the seabed also contain preserved roots and soil from ancient forests.

ICE INVADERS

The *Noto* arrives in the Bellingshausen Sea, and the dive team plunges into an otherworldly soundscape. Under the ice it sounds like a battle of alien spaceships is raging, with laser guns firing all around them. In fact, it's another of Antarctica's special animals.

Oscar sets up an underwater hydrophone and camera to learn more about why seals make these noises.

Pew pew!

Weddell seals make some very high-pitched sounds, too high for humans to hear by themselves.

Trill!

Even when Weddell seals are on the ice, they can still hear the sounds of other seals underwater.

Secret sounds

The seals are noisier during Antarctica's dark months, so it's possible they use their sonar to help them find prey and to locate breathing holes in the ice when there's no light to see by.

Seals might also be using sonar to talk to each other while trying not to let predators, like orca, eavesdrop on their conversations. The high-pitched sounds don't travel far through the water so hunters are less likely to hear them.

Weddell seal
Leptonychotes weddellii

Size: 11 feet
Lifespan: 30 years
🆔 Least Concern

Weddell seals can hold their breath for more than an hour and dive deeper than almost 2,000 feet.

Chirp!

They have extremely sensitive whiskers, called vibrissae, which help them catch prey at close range.

– Thurston Island –

Named after W. Harris Thurston who designed the windproof cloth used on Antarctic expeditions in the 1940s.

CLIMATE CONTROLLER

Antarctica's huge, icy continent is vital for the rest of planet Earth.
Without it, life everywhere would be completely different.

Moving heat and cold

The coldest, saltiest water anywhere on Earth forms around
Antarctica. It's very dense and quickly sinks to the bottom of the
sea—scientists call it Antarctic Bottom Water. This cold, salty water
feeds into a huge underwater current that spirals around Antarctica
and swirls like a giant conveyor belt mixing up the whole ocean.

*Antarctic Bottom Water is a driving
force for the global current.*

Without this current, the equator would get hotter, and the
poles would get colder. The current moves heat through the
ocean and into the air above. It makes many parts of the world
the right temperature for life to thrive—including humans.

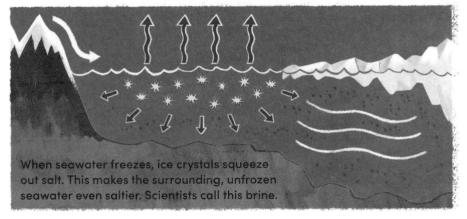

When seawater freezes, ice crystals squeeze out salt. This makes the surrounding, unfrozen seawater even saltier. Scientists call this brine.

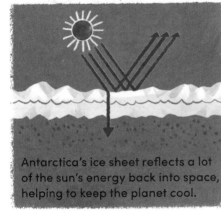

Antarctica's ice sheet reflects a lot of the sun's energy back into space, helping to keep the planet cool.

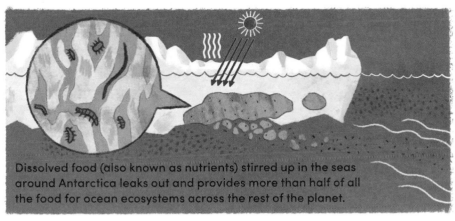

Dissolved food (also known as nutrients) stirred up in the seas around Antarctica leaks out and provides more than half of all the food for ocean ecosystems across the rest of the planet.

The Southern Ocean takes up a lot of carbon; in the water, in animals and in the seabed.

But because of climate change, Antarctica is changing.

Temperatures are going up faster in parts of Antarctica than most of the rest of the planet, both in the air and in the ocean. Scientists are studying how the animals living on and around Antarctica will cope with the warmer temperatures.

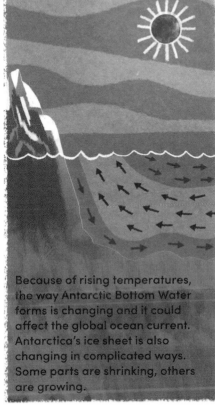

Because of rising temperatures, the way Antarctic Bottom Water forms is changing and it could affect the global ocean current. Antarctica's ice sheet is also changing in complicated ways. Some parts are shrinking, others are growing.

The Southern Ocean is getting more acidic, because when carbon dioxide from the atmosphere dissolves in seawater it forms acid. This makes it difficult for many sea creatures to survive, like tiny swimming snails called sea butterflies.

HOW LONG UNTIL DOOMSDAY?

Greenhouse gases are building up gradually and trapping the sun's heat in the atmosphere, and scientists are worried this could trigger very fast changes in Antarctica. The *Noto* arrives in the Amundsen Sea where Ari sends the AUV, *Mirounga*, on a mission underneath the enormous Thwaites Glacier. It also goes by the nickname the "Doomsday Glacier."

If Thwaites Glacier collapses, the ice sheet could suddenly slump into the ocean and a lot of it would melt quickly.

As air temperatures and sea temperatures warm up because of climate change, some ice shelves around Antarctica are melting from the top and from the bottom. This is happening on Thwaites Glacier. Ice scientists are very worried because the glacier acts like a giant plug, holding back a massive part of Antarctica's ice sheet behind it.

The water melting from Thwaites Glacier could cause sea levels around the world to rise by 2 feet. This may not sound like a lot, but it would cause flooding in lots of island nations and big cities. Around one in ten people today live less than 33 feet above sea level.

Mirounga monitors Thwaites Glacier to help figure out how soon it's likely to collapse, and if it does, just how bad it could be for the rest of the planet.

PIONEERING WOMEN IN ANTARCTICA

These are the Dry Valleys of Antarctica. As their name suggests, they are one of the driest places in Antarctica, and anywhere on Earth. It hasn't rained here for two million years! Any snow that falls evaporates very quickly in the dry wind. It's such an extreme desert that many scientists have come here to study very old ice, the rocks, and glaciers, and even how bacteria can survive inside rocks.

In 1969, American geologist Lois Jones led the first all-woman team of scientists in Antarctica. The team was Kay Lindsay (an insect specialist), Terry Lee Tickhill (a chemist), and Eileen McSaveney (another geologist). They went to the Dry Valleys to study how the rocks interact with melting ice, and how this might impact wildlife living further downstream.

Lois's team spent four months in Antarctica. While they were there, she asked if she could fly on a supply plane heading to a US Navy base at the South Pole, so she could get a good look at the rocky landscape from the air.

The men in charge of the flight decided it was best if nobody could claim to be the first woman at the South Pole. Lois and her team, together with a female journalist and another scientist who joined them, were told to step off the plane at the same time (alongside Rear Admiral David F. Welch from the US Navy). So they all arrived together! These were the first six women to set foot at the South Pole.

The Dry Valleys are home to many very salty lakes and Antarctica's longest river—a meltwater stream, 19 miles long, called the Onyx River.

THE WORLD'S SMALLEST ORCA

The *Noto* sails into the Ross Sea and stops in Terra Nova Bay, where the team watches and listens for some local top predators.

Orca calls

The Ross Sea is home to the world's smallest orcas, known as type C (other types of Antarctic orca are called A, B1, B2 and D). When Oscar spies a pod of type C orcas swimming off the edge of the ice, he lowers a hydrophone to record their calls. They are easy to identify from above the water, but he plans to find out what the orca sound like when they're diving underwater out of sight.

Tck tck tck!

– Terra Nova Bay –

The bay was named after a British sailing ship that brought explorers to Antarctica in the early 20th century.

Oscar listens for three main types of orca call. There are short pulses of sound, called clicks, which last for several seconds. Orcas use these for echolocation, to find prey and to navigate. To communicate with each other, orcas whistle for a few seconds at a time, and they also emit faster clicks, called burst-pulses.

Eeeeeeee!

Underwater listening station

Oscar's recordings show that type C orca have their own distinct calls that are different from the other orcas. It means now he can leave hydrophones underwater in a listening station to monitor the orca population all year in these remote, protected waters of Antarctica.

Type C orca are fish-eaters and are easily identified by their white slanted eye patch.

Orca
Orcinus orca

Size: 20 feet–31 feet
Lifespan: 30–60 years
(?) Unassessed

BZZZZZZZZ!

The Ross Sea region Marine Protected Area was set up in December 2019. For thirty-five years, fishing will not be allowed in about 640,930 mi² of the sea to protect the fragile, icy ecosystem.

Orcas A, B, C, and D are known as ecotypes. Scientists think they are probably all the same species, even though they look different from each other.

Type A

Type B

Type C

Type D

45

SPACE WEATHER

Lara and Ari leave the *Noto* for a while and fly towards the South Pole to study the beautiful polar lights. Swirling green curtains glimmer in the sky. These polar lights are caused by what scientists call space weather.

Space weather is just like the weather we all know well but it happens much higher up, in the part of space closest to Earth. There's no air or atmosphere up there, but a soup of electrically charged particles. This is called the magnetosphere.

In Antarctica, the polar lights are known as aurora australis. In the Arctic, they are known as aurora borealis.

Huge explosions on the surface of the sun send out masses of charged particles which hurtle through space at around almost 250 million miles per hour. When they crash into the Earth's magnetosphere they cause vast geomagnetic storms. Sometimes super-fast particles plummet even closer to Earth and crash into gases in the upper atmosphere. They light up the sky in different colors and cause the polar lights, or aurora.

Sun

Magnetosphere

Earth

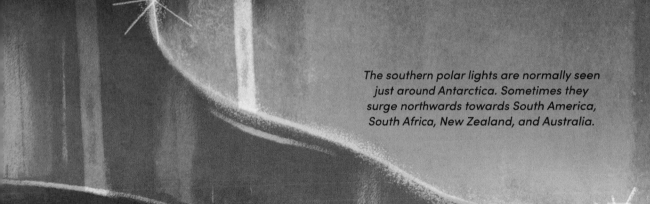

The southern polar lights are normally seen just around Antarctica. Sometimes they surge northwards towards South America, South Africa, New Zealand, and Australia.

The space weather forecast

Lara is interested in geomagnetic storms because they can stop satellites working and trigger electricity blackouts by upsetting power grids.

She takes measurements using instruments set up all around Antarctica, including here at the South Pole. She works with scientists all around the world to make space weather forecasts!

Polar lights happen near the north and south magnetic poles, where the lines of the Earth's magnetic fields bunch together.

– Geographic South Pole –

This is the southern tip of an imaginary line (or axis) which the Earth spins around, like a spinning top. The Geographic South Pole always stays in the same place.

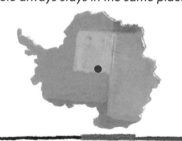

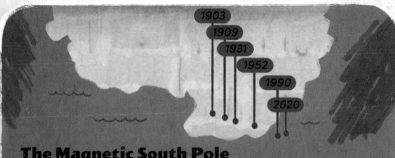

1903
1909
1931
1952
1990
2020

The Magnetic South Pole

This is where the lines of the Earth's magnetic fields all join together. If you hold a magnetic compass directly over the South Pole, the needle would try to point straight down towards the ground. The magnetic south pole doesn't stay in the same place.

QUEST FOR THE OLDEST ICE

High up on the Antarctic Plateau, around 620 miles from the edges of the continent, there's a summit sticking up in the ice sheet called Dome C. Here the ice sheet is especially thick and old. Ari and Lara fly to Dome C to meet scientists from the nearby research base and help drill a long core of ice, which will let them work out what the Earth's climate was like a very long time ago.

Ari carefully takes small samples of the ice from the core back to the lab, to melt them and measure chemicals that were dissolved in the ice. These chemicals will show what the temperature was back when the ice formed, and the amount of dust in the air—which helps them understand what the climate used to be like around Antarctica.

Time travel in Antarctica

Drilling down into the ice sheet is like going back in time. Falling snow builds up and gets squashed into ice under its own weight. As the ice layers build up every year they trap air bubbles. These bubbles record what the Earth's atmosphere used to be like, including how much carbon dioxide gas there was. At Dome C there are layers of ice going back 800,000 years. In all that time they haven't been crushed and mixed up but stayed in neat layers.

Reaching even further back in time

The scientists at Dome C are drilling a core around 1.86 miles long down into the ice. It's taking a very long time! They're hoping to drill far enough down to reach ice that is over a million years old—older than any ice that's been drilled before. This will help show what was happening during an important time in Earth's history when the climate was changing dramatically at the start of a great ice age.

Knowing what happened to the climate in the past is important for predicting the future, as more greenhouse gases build up in the atmosphere.

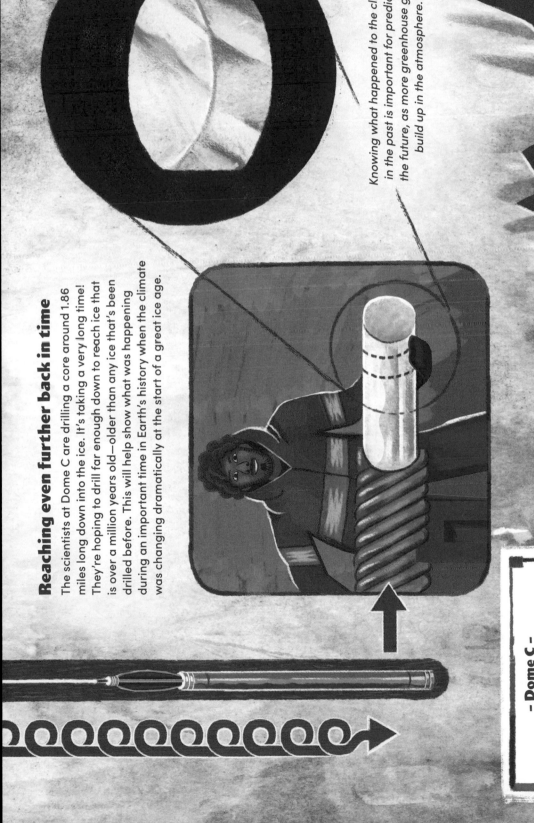

– Dome C –
Dome C is located 2 miles above sea level.

SPYING A RARE MARVEL IN THE DEEP

Back together on the *Noto*, the team sails into the Mawson Sea where Michelle takes down the deep-diving submersible, *Kiwa*, with a special glowing light fixed to the outside. She hopes this will lure a mysterious creature of the deep cold Southern Ocean that has rarely been seen alive.

Glowing lure

The light is designed to look like a jellyfish which flashes when it's attacked by a predator. The idea is it will attract an even bigger predator—a colossal squid. These giant cephalopods don't eat jellyfish, but they do eat things that eat jellyfish, which is probably why they come to investigate.

Michelle waits patiently until she sees enormous tentacles reaching out of the dark. She films the colossal squid and later she will watch the footage and learn more about these mysterious animals.

Polar giants

At just under 1,120 pounds in weight, colossal squid are the world's heaviest invertebrates (animals that don't have a backbone). It's another case of polar gigantism, like giant sea spiders.

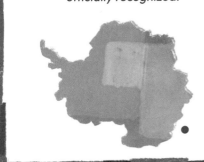

– Mawson Sea –

This is one of many places in Antarctica with names that haven't yet been officially recognized.

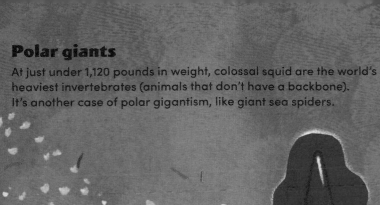

Colossal squid
Mesonychoteuthis hamiltoni

Size: About 30 feet
Lifespan: Unknown
LC Least Concern

Colossal squid also have the largest eyes on the planet, just over 10 inches across—bigger than a basketball. And their eyes glow in the dark! Bacteria around each eye produce light via a chemical reaction. No one is quite sure, but the squid may use their eyes as headlights to see through the dark water.

SEAL SEARCHING

In the Davis Sea, along the coast of East Antarctica, Captain Nyree carefully steers the *Noto* through open cracks in the pack ice. Ari sends up a drone to monitor the ice from above to help find a safe passage and take pictures which will help the scientists understand how the ice is changing over time. Meanwhile, Oscar surveys the seals that lie at the edges of the pack ice as the ship passes by.

Gaps in the ice are important for seals and whales to breathe.

Leopard seal
Hydrurga leptonyx

Size: 11.5 feet
Lifespan: 25 years
(LC) Least Concern

– Davis Sea –

If you sailed north from the Davis Sea for 4,971 miles, the next land you would reach is Sri Lanka.

Crabeater seal
Lobodon carcinophaga

Size: 8 miles
Lifespan: 40 years (average 20)
ⓛⓒ Least Concern

The language of ice

Ice formations have different names in Antarctica, depending on the size.

Icebergs: *stand at least 16 feet above sea level, area at least 5,382 ft².*

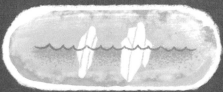

Bergy bits: *chunks broken off icebergs, 3–16.5 feet above sea level, area up to 3,329 ft².*

Growlers: *smaller chunks, less than 4 feet above sea level, area less than 216 ft².*

Brash ice: *ice chunks smaller than 7 feet across.*

Pancake ice: *newly forming sea ice that look like pancakes!*

Polynyas: *Ice-free areas of sea, often roughly oval or circular in shape.*

Leads: *long, narrow cracks in sea ice.*

ANIMAL SCIENTISTS

The *Noto* team heads away from the Antarctic continent to a group of islands in the east. Ji-hae is investigating how seawater moves through the complicated channels and peaks on the seafloor, as a strong undersea current crashes into the Kerguelen Islands. But she needs a little help from her friends!

Seal science assistants

Ji-hae and Oscar carefully glue a special sensor to the heads of elephant seals. As the seals swim around finding their food, the sensors record the water's saltiness and temperature and how deep the seal swims. Ji-hae will use this information to understand how seawater is moving through the small gaps between the islands.

Their sensor "hats" don't cause the seals any harm. They will drop off after a few months when the seals shed their fur.

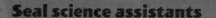

Macaroni penguin
Eudyptes chrysolophus

Size: 27.5 inches
Lifespan: 12 years
(V) Vulnerable

Southern rockhopper penguin
Leudyptes chrysocome

Size: 22 inches
Lifespan: 10 years
(V) Vulnerable

The *Noto* team spots some penguin species that they haven't seen so far. Rockhoppers and macaroni penguins are not found on the Antarctic continent but do live on the nearby islands, including the Kerguelens.

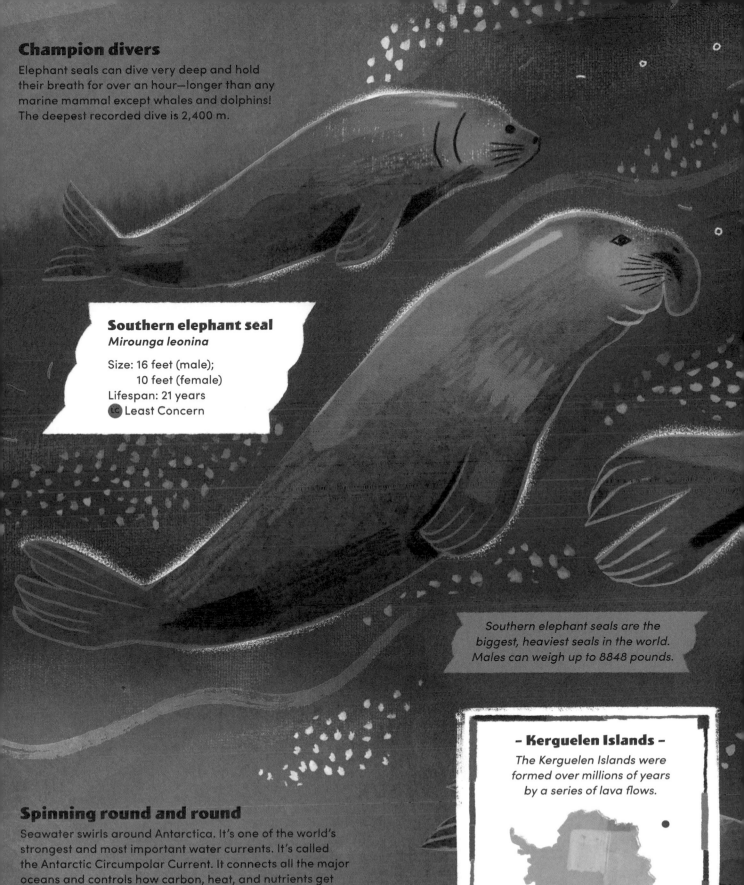

Champion divers

Elephant seals can dive very deep and hold their breath for over an hour—longer than any marine mammal except whales and dolphins! The deepest recorded dive is 2,400 m.

Southern elephant seal
Mirounga leonina

Size: 16 feet (male);
      10 feet (female)
Lifespan: 21 years
🅛🅒 Least Concern

Southern elephant seals are the biggest, heaviest seals in the world. Males can weigh up to 8848 pounds.

– Kerguelen Islands –

The Kerguelen Islands were formed over millions of years by a series of lava flows.

Spinning round and round

Seawater swirls around Antarctica. It's one of the world's strongest and most important water currents. It's called the Antarctic Circumpolar Current. It connects all the major oceans and controls how carbon, heat, and nutrients get stored down in the deep sea. Scientists working all around the Southern Ocean gather data so together they can understand better how this current works.

THE TWILIGHT ZONE

The ocean's Twilight Zone lies between 656 and 3,280 feet underwater. Scientists know very little about this part of the ocean—especially in the Southern Ocean. Off the coast of Dronning Maud Land, Michelle sends down large nets into the Twilight Zone to study fish with lights twinkling along their bellies.

Lanternfish live in enormous shoals. During the day they swim around the Twilight Zone and at night they rise towards the surface where they hunt for plankton and krill. Like krill, lanternfish are important in Southern Ocean food webs—they get eaten by penguins, seals and whales.

Lanternfish
Myctophids

Size: 0.5–8 inches
Lifespan: 2.5–5 years
(?) Unassessed

- Dronning Maud Land -
Dronning Maud Land was named after Queen Maud of Norway.

Shrinking fish

Michelle measures the temperature of the water where different lanternfish live. She finds that the biggest species live in the coldest water. For lanternfish, it could cause problems as the Southern Ocean keeps on getting warmer. In future, only smaller lanternfish may survive here, and bigger lanternfish could die out or move somewhere else. If that happens, the predators in the Southern Ocean that eat lanternfish might find it hard to get enough food, if all they can find to eat are smaller lanternfish which contain less energy.

Hiding behind the light

The lanternfishes's belly lights give them a cloak of invisibility. By glowing blue, they match the dim light that surrounds them in the Twilight Zone. Predators swimming underneath don't see the fish-shaped silhouette of a lanternfish.

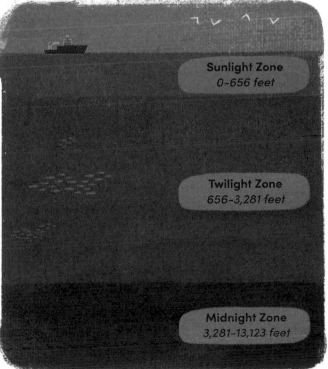

Sunlight Zone
0–656 feet

Twilight Zone
656–3,281 feet

Midnight Zone
3,281–13,123 feet

World's most common fish

Lanternfish live in the Twilight Zone all around the world. There are far too many to count all of them. There are probably hundreds of trillions, more than any other fish in the ocean.

ICE WALKERS

With the *Noto* moored off the coast of Dronning Maud Land, Javier and Jojo hike across the sea ice of Atka Bay. In the distance, thousands of emperor penguins are waddling along, returning from months of hunting for fish and krill at sea. The penguins are heading back to their colony on the sea ice as they do every year. To monitor the penguin colony without getting too close, Jojo has brought along a special gadget.

Watching penguins with robo-eyes

A small robot trundles over the ice, steering all by itself. It has cameras and sensors that track penguin numbers and movements, and sends data to the research station standing on the ice nearby. Jojo will leave the robot to keep an eye on the penguins as they complete the next stages of their life cycle.

Feathered sentinels

Emperor penguins are key animals in Antarctica. By monitoring them and seeing how they are coping with climate change, scientists are learning about the health of the entire ecosystem.

Emperor penguin
Aptenodytes forsteri

Height: 3 feet
Lifespan: 20 years
NT Near Threatened

The emperor penguin life cycle

1. Females lay their eggs and carefully pass them to their mates—the exposed eggs can easily freeze on the ice. Then the females go back to sea to feed.

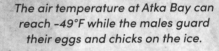

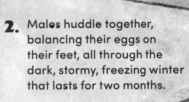

2. Males huddle together, balancing their eggs on their feet, all through the dark, stormy, freezing winter that lasts for two months.

The air temperature at Atka Bay can reach -49°F while the males guard their eggs and chicks on the ice.

3. Finally the sun rises again and the fluffy chicks hatch.

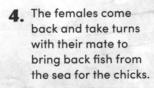

4. The females come back and take turns with their mate to bring back fish from the sea for the chicks.

5. When they're big enough, the chicks shed and grow sleek adult feathers. Then they're ready to plunge into the Southern Ocean.

There are sixty-one emperor penguin colonies around Antarctica. If greenhouse gas emissions aren't cut fast enough, 80% of them could disappear by the end of the century because the ice shelves will collapse as temperatures rise. But if greenhouse gases are successfully reduced, only between 19 and 31% of the colonies will be lost.

KINGDOM OF THE ICEFISH

In the Weddell Sea, the team tows an underwater video camera behind the *Noto* to study what lives under the ice. Suddenly they see something nobody was expecting. The entire seabed is dotted with thousands of perfect, round nests. On each one is a crocodile icefish.

There's nest after nest after nest. Sitting on their nests, every fish guards around 1,700 blue eggs.

Jonah's crocodile icefish
Neopagetopsis ionah

Size: 22 inches
Lifespan: Unknown
(?) Unassessed

The team keeps on towing the camera above the seabed. They figure out that the icefish colony covers at least 100 mi² and contains a mind-blowing 60 million nests. It's the biggest colony of fish nests found anywhere in the ocean!

Michelle attaches a camera to the seabed to watch the eggs as they hatch and see whether the fish come back to the same nests every year.

Together, all these fish weigh more than 66,1389 tons, the same as 10,000 male African elephants.

1,500 Weddell seals can be found in the area which hunt the nesting fish.

Now and then, giant sea spiders dart in and grab eggs from the nests.

– Weddell Sea –

The Weddell Sea is named after Scottish sailor James Weddell who sailed there in 1823.

ANIMALS MADE OF GLASS

Next the *Noto* heads to Pudsey Bay in the Weddell Sea, where Michelle takes *Kiwa* down 656.17 feet to explore what looks like a strange forest spread across the deep seafloor. Enigmatic creatures grow there in all sorts of shapes and sizes like peculiar plants and mushrooms, but in fact they're animals called sponges. They sit quite still and pump huge amounts of seawater through their bodies, filtering tiny particles of food. Michelle surveys the sponge reef to see what species live there.

Sponges provide shelter and food for lots of other creatures. Some species of sponge can live for hundreds and thousands of years!

Volcano sponge
Anoxycalyx joubini

Size: 7 feet tall, 3 feet wide
Lifespan: perhaps as long as 15,000 years!
⦵ Unassessed

Laura's sponge
Doconesthes robinsoni

Size: total size unknown
Lifespan: unknown
⦵ Unassessed

Who is who?

Sponge species are very difficult to identify just by looking at them or photographing them. Sometimes the same species can grow in completely different shapes. Michelle uses *Kiwa*'s robotic arm to carefully snip small bits of sponge to bring back to the *Noto*. But she has to be careful—sponges start to stink after they're fished out of the sea and brought up on deck!

Many sponges' skeletons are made out of tiny pieces of glass, called spicules, that come in lots of different shapes. Back in the lab, Michelle looks at the spicules with a microscope to figure out which species she has found.

Uncovering glass sponge reefs

Ice shelves around Antarctica are collapsing and scientists are now able to study glass sponge reefs that used to be hidden under the ice. The disappearing ice is transforming the underwater world and sponges are quickly changing. Some sponge reefs are getting much bigger because there's more sunlight reaching the water and more tiny algae growing for sponges to feed on. Scientists will keep monitoring the reefs to see how they respond to their changing environment.

FINDING HOPE ON DEVIL ISLAND

At their final stop in the Weddell Sea, the *Noto* team calls in at Devil Island where they make an uplifting discovery.

They count the chicks of the ice-loving Adélie penguins. There are 21,500. This is really good news! It's a similar number to the last time scientists counted them here a decade ago. The colony of Adélie penguins is not shrinking like others are over on the Antarctic Peninsula.

Adélie penguins depend on sea ice. They climb onto it to rest in between deep dives when they go fishing. This is where they sit while they shed their feathers and stay out of the sea until a new, waterproof layer grows.

Adélie penguin
Pygoscelis adeliae

Size: 28 inches
Lifespan: 10–20 years
LC Least Concern

Following penguins

To understand more about how these Adélies are coping as Antarctica warms up, Jojo and Javier launch a glider, which looks like a small, underwater airplane. It glides along, using very little battery power, and follows the penguins as they dive into deep underwater canyons. The scientists want to know more about how the Adélies go fishing.

The glider measures temperature and chemicals in the water, and detects blooms of algae and swarms of krill. Javier and Jojo will use this data to draw up plans for protecting the most important parts of the Southern Ocean from huge fishing boats that come to Antarctica to catch krill. Protecting krill will help ensure Adélie penguins and other Antarctic animals have enough to eat and survive into the future.

INVASION OF ANTARCTICA!

The team heads off the northern tip of the Antarctic Peninsula to the South Orkney Islands. Javier leaves the *Noto* for a few days to study plants and animals on Signy Island.

Annual meadow grass
Poa annua

Size: 6–10 inches

Annual meadow grass grows all around the world but only recently arrived in sub-Antarctic islands.

New arrivals

Antarctica has been isolated for millions of years and unique creatures have evolved to live on the continent. Now that more people are traveling here, for holidays or work, some of them accidentally bring species from other places. There can be seeds stuck to their clothes and boots, insects hiding in food or equipment, and sea creatures stuck onto the outside of boats. These invasive species, as people call them, can cause trouble in Antarctic ecosystems, especially as temperatures warm due to global climate change.

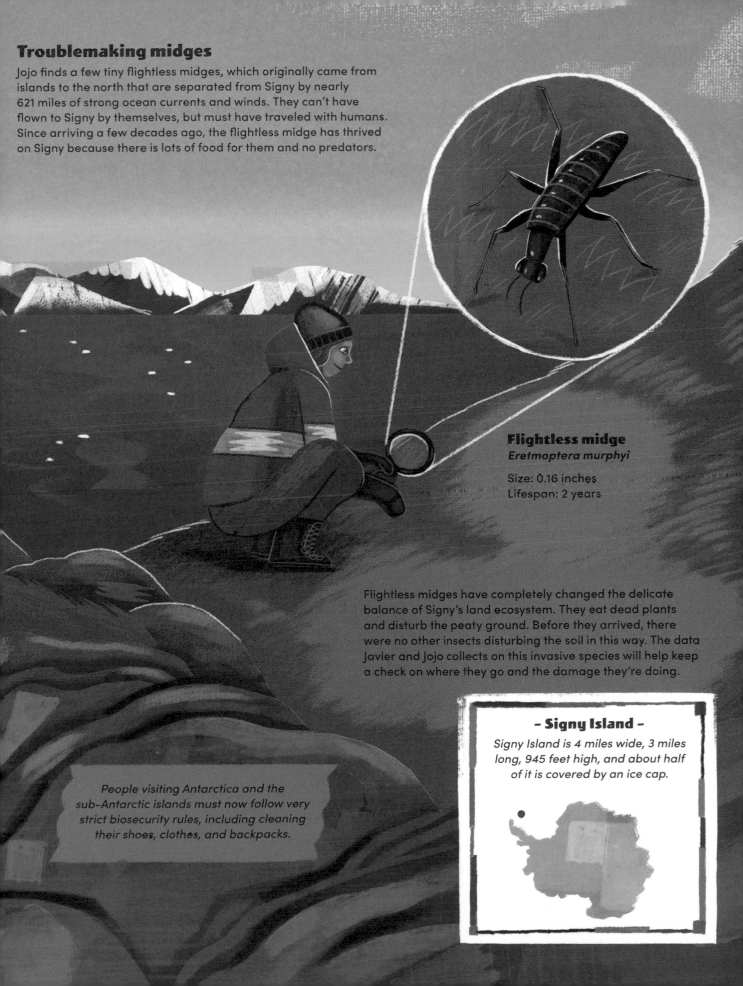

Troublemaking midges

Jojo finds a few tiny flightless midges, which originally came from islands to the north that are separated from Signy by nearly 621 miles of strong ocean currents and winds. They can't have flown to Signy by themselves, but must have traveled with humans. Since arriving a few decades ago, the flightless midge has thrived on Signy because there is lots of food for them and no predators.

Flightless midge
Eretmoptera murphyi

Size: 0.16 inches
Lifespan: 2 years

Flightless midges have completely changed the delicate balance of Signy's land ecosystem. They eat dead plants and disturb the peaty ground. Before they arrived, there were no other insects disturbing the soil in this way. The data Javier and Jojo collects on this invasive species will help keep a check on where they go and the damage they're doing.

People visiting Antarctica and the sub-Antarctic islands must now follow very strict biosecurity rules, including cleaning their shoes, clothes, and backpacks.

– Signy Island –

Signy Island is 4 miles wide, 3 miles long, 945 feet high, and about half of it is covered by an ice cap.

THE BLUE GIANTS ARE BACK

As the *Noto* team arrives at the island of South Georgia, Oscar looks for some of the biggest animals that have ever lived.

South Georgia is an important place for blue whales. There used to be many of them swimming around until last century when people, mostly from Britain, came here to hunt whales. Their enormous bodies were hauled onshore and their blubber was boiled down to make into margarine, soap, glue, and lipstick. People only stopped hunting whales around South Georgia when there were none left to find. Now, all that's left behind are the rusting buildings of the abandoned factories.

– South Georgia Island –

South Georgia Island has a population of thirty-two scientists in summer and sixteen in winter.

Antarctic blue whale
Balaenoptera musculus intermedia

Size: 98 feet
Lifespan: 80–90 years
EN Endangered

Missing whales

Even after whaling stopped, blue whales were missing from South Georgia for decades. Between 1998 and 2018, scientists went looking for blue whales around South Georgia and only saw one. Then in 2020, a team of scientists spotted fifty-eight of these huge giants. The blue whales of South Georgia are back!

Now scientists, including Oscar, come to South Georgia to monitor the blue whales and keep an eye on how they're doing.

Between 1904 and 1971, people killed 42,698 blue whales off South Georgia.

Hunting whales has been banned around the world since 1982, except for indigenous hunts in a few countries. Some countries continue to kill whales for scientific purposes, even though there are now lots of clever ways to study whales without killing them.

BOUNTY ON BIRD ISLAND

Off the north-west tip of South Georgia, the ship makes a final stop and calls in at Bird Island. This small island is one of the richest places for wildlife in the world and there's plenty for the *Noto* team to be doing.

Wandering albatross have the largest wingspan of any bird.

Wandering albatross
Diomedea exulans

Wingspan: 11 feet
Lifespan: 50 years
Ⓥ Vulnerable

Seabirds in danger

Javier surveys the wandering albatross, which are busy rearing their chicks. Numbers of albatross are decreasing because the adults get caught on fishing lines as they fly across the ocean to feed. Colorful lines attached to fishing lines help to scare the birds away, so not as many get caught and drown.

Grey-headed albatross
Thalassarche chrysostoma

Wingspan: 7 feet
Lifespan: 35 years
ⒺⓃ Endangered

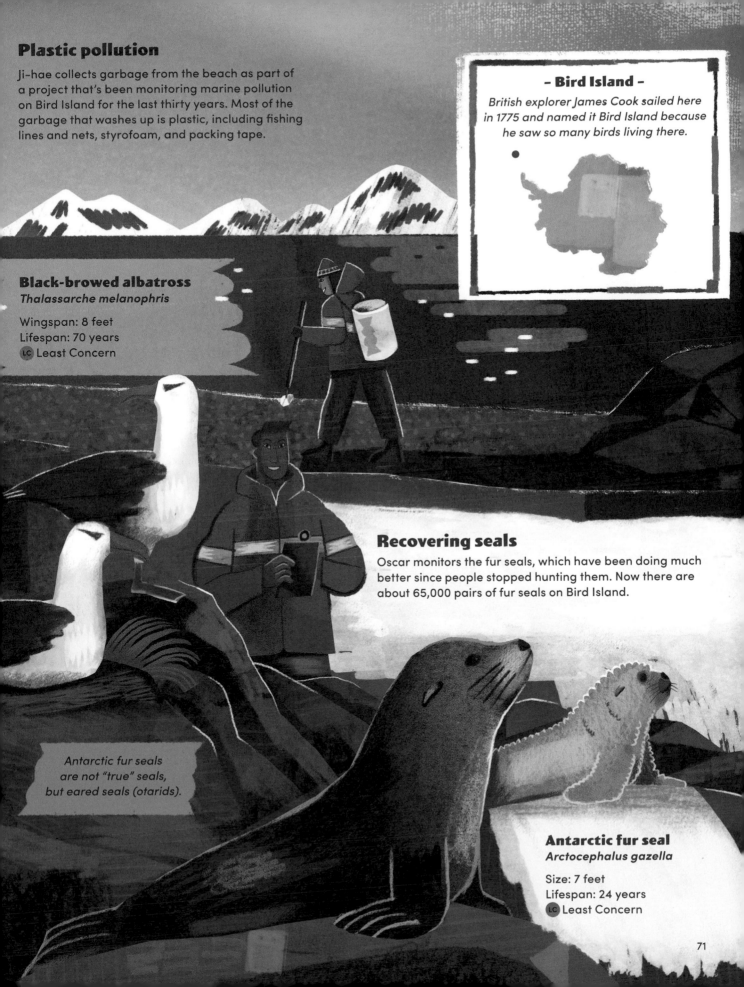

Plastic pollution

Ji-hae collects garbage from the beach as part of a project that's been monitoring marine pollution on Bird Island for the last thirty years. Most of the garbage that washes up is plastic, including fishing lines and nets, styrofoam, and packing tape.

– Bird Island –

British explorer James Cook sailed here in 1775 and named it Bird Island because he saw so many birds living there.

Black-browed albatross
Thalassarche melanophris

Wingspan: 8 feet
Lifespan: 70 years
LC Least Concern

Recovering seals

Oscar monitors the fur seals, which have been doing much better since people stopped hunting them. Now there are about 65,000 pairs of fur seals on Bird Island.

Antarctic fur seals are not "true" seals, but eared seals (otarids).

Antarctic fur seal
Arctocephalus gazella

Size: 7 feet
Lifespan: 24 years
LC Least Concern

STEAMING HOME

The *Noto* leaves Antarctica behind and as it steams north the team of scientists is busy getting everything organized. After the expedition has finished, the team meets to tell people about the fragile, icy world of Antarctica.

WHAT NEXT FOR ANTARCTICA?

The future of Antarctica, and all its amazing wildlife, depends on the choices people around the world make in the next few years. If we look after Antarctica and manage to reduce the greenhouse gases we release into the atmosphere . . .

. . . we can limit the rise in air and ocean temperatures, so fewer of the ice shelves and glaciers will melt . . .

. . . we can limit the loss of Antarctica's sea ice, and help protect the species that depend on the ice to survive . . .

. . . we can limit the sea-level rise caused by the melting of the ice sheet in Antarctica . . .

. . . we can protect more of the ocean around Antarctica from fishing, and make sure there's enough food for penguins, whales, seals, and birds to eat . . .

. . . and we can limit the invasion of alien species that could damage the ecosystems around the continent.

. . . we can limit how acidic the oceans become, and limit the damage to sea creatures . . .

If we work together, we can help protect Antarctica's environment and ecosystems so that they can be healthy in the future. This will be good not just for the creatures the *Noto* team met along the way, but for everyone on the planet.

GLOSSARY

A

Antifreeze: A substance that prevents liquids from freezing

Archipelago: A collection of islands

C

Continent: A large, solid area of land. The Earth has seven continents. Asia, Africa, North America, South America, Antarctica, Europe, and Australia

Crustacean: Animals like crabs or lobsters, that have a hard covering, called an exoskeleton, to their bodies

Currents: A body of fluid like water, or air, moving in a specific direction

E

Ecosystem: All the living things, including plants and animals, that live in a certain area

Echolocation: A technique used by some animals, like bats and dolphins, to locate objects using reflected sound

Equator: The imaginary line around the Earth that separates the northern and southern halves, or hemispheres

Evolve: To develop or change by steps

F

Fossil fuels: Natural substances like coal or gas, which humans burn for fuel

G

Glacier: Huge, thick masses of ice

Greenhouse gases: Gases in the Earth's atmosphere that trap heat from the sun near the Earth's surface

H

Hydrophone: An instrument for listening to sound transmitted through water

I

Invasive species: A species that has been introduced to an area that it doesn't naturally belong to and causes it harm

M

Migration: When animals move on a regular cycle

P

Peninsula: A body of land surrounded by water on three sides

S

Sample: A part or thing that shows the quality of the whole or group

Single-use plastic: Plastic products that can only be used once before they are thrown away

Shoal: A place where a sea, lake or river is shallow, also a group of fish swimming together

Sonar: A way to find objects underwater by sending and reflecting sound waves

Species: A group that contains all of a certain type of animal, plant or other organism with the same characteristics

T

Territory: The area an animal lives in, which they may defend from other animals

Z

Zero carbon: Something that produces no carbon emissions

INDEX

Written by Helen Scales _and_ Kate Hendry

Dr Helen Scales is a writer, marine biologist, broadcaster, and scuba diver whose work focuses on the ocean and its inhabitants. She has a masters degree in Tropical Coastal Management from Newcastle University, and a PhD from Cambridge University, UK.

Professor Kate Hendry is a polar scientist who has lived for almost two years in total in the Arctic and Antarctica. She has been chief scientist on research ships and studies the impacts of climate change on seawater and algae in the ocean.

Helen and Kate are sisters who grew up exploring the coast together.

Illustrated by Rômolo D'Hipólito

Rômolo D'Hipólito is a Brazilian artist and illustrator. In 2019, he received the Special Mention Award at Golden Pinwheel Young Illustrators Competition, and in 2018, he was selected for the Ibero-America official catalog. Other works by Rômolo include the illustrated guide _Earth's Incredible Places: Amazon River_. Beyond publishing, his creative pursuits involve painting, sculpture, comics and animation.

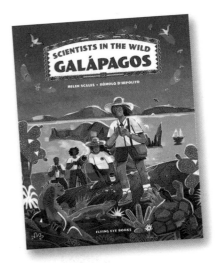

Also in the series . . .

Join a team of scientists as they set sail around the Galápagos Islands. Tasked with observing and protecting the islands' amazing wildlife, the scientists will track and study the animals and plants that are unique to this incredible archipelago. To get the job done they will climb volcanoes, get sneezed on by marine iguanas, launch a deep-diving submersible, and explore the dazzling underwater wonders of the Galápagos.